G
Rave

I

Mark Cunningham

Mark Young

harry k stammer

Sandy Press 2025

G
Rave

I

Cover art by harry k stammer

Published by Sandy Press (sandy-press.com)

ISBN-13: 979-8-9924582-0-6

Introduction

Gravel. Might have been called that because it was like walking over it in bare feet to get three grumpy old men to agree on how this book should be put together — identifiers or anonymous; interspersed small offerings or a three-tiered cake; with or without an intro?

Or? Call it that because it's a word with other, quite divergent, words built in & easily accessed — rave, ave, grave, Ravel — & that's before discarding the original order.

Or? Each of the pieces, as denoted by the poet's name, being inserted into the document in a random way, like gravel on a path. The point here is to cross each author's approach in a way that does or doesn't affect the how of how the pieces relate to each other. Does this matter in terms of how a reader understands each alone & at the same time how a reader may understand the whole & the poetry within the total work?

Or? What is there to introduce? *The Pisan Cantos* and Zukofsky's *A* made do without introductions, if I recall. Maybe when you're famous—or post-famous, so that people need to be told how important you are. Were. Is that "you" plural? Or, as with Aram Saroyan's *Complete Minimal Poems*, you can have a blurb with more words in it than most of the books included. Then you can get somebody to write an introduction to tell us who the blurb writer, Vito Acconci, is. Was. Who will introduce the introducer?

Or? The only true blurb would be along the lines of: "If you read this book and get irritated as hell & say to yourself, 'Anybody could do that,' then you're got the real spirit of the book."

Take all of the above, & it's no wonder they invited me in to compose the introduction. All suggestions will be welcomed. Keep watching this space.

— Kasimir Malevich, February ~~1915~~ 2025, Red Square

summerde

.

pl ant

.

JET PLANE

c loud

googoogle

.

randumb

After Magritte

ADAM DAG

DAMD AGA

MAGA DAD

AMGD ADA

MAGD AAD

ADGA AMD

DADA MAG

La Joconde

```
        da
     Vinc      i
    would      be
    pleased    that
    Magritte   has
    managed    to
    capture    the
    enigma     tic
     smile     so
     well      .
```

Memory

```
S O U V E N I R
S O U V E N I
S O U V E N
S O U V E       R
S O U V     E R
S O U     I E R
S O     L I E R
S     B L I E R
    U B L I E R
  O U B L I E R
```

Disco

Vert't

Disco Ver't

I
o

noctorn

.

sleap

flew id

.

REMember

PVS

per

ver
ser

powerflot

The little old lady who
may be a cliché but
not this particular
little old lady nor
this particular
roll of the
dice.

l||\\||//||//||\\\\||\\||ibra
ry

*

sem{if}inal

*

rat : o

*

contemptlate

*

```
                a
           n
      g
           l
                e
```

*

egotesticle

*

innocentive

*

orthodon'tist

*

ambidextrose

*

29	30
Cu	Zn

Fug

It

I've

Fug It I've

Po

TA

toes

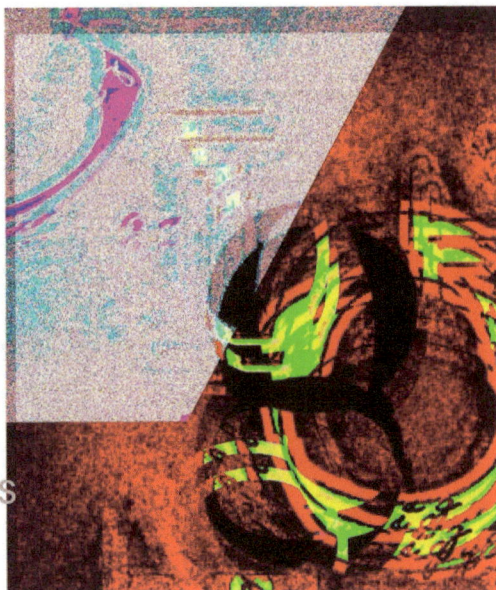

Po TA toes

Cea

Sars

Di

Et

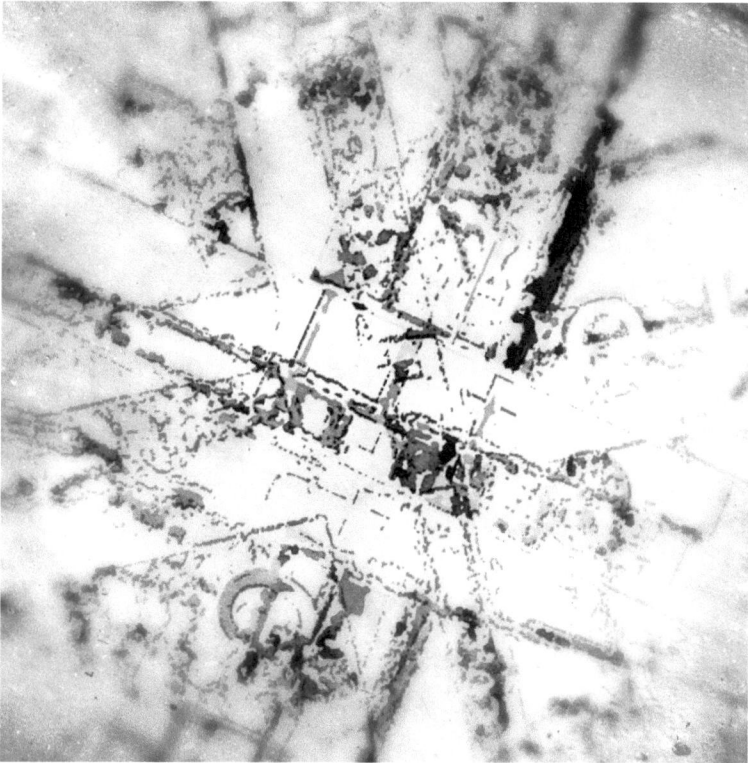

AFTER READING A POEM BY
ROBERT BLY IN WHCH HE STEPS
INTO A ROOM WHERE HE EXPECTS
TO FIND SOMEONE ONLY FOR THE
PERSON NOT TO BE THERE AND
ROBERT IS SURPRISED, I STEP INTO
A ROOM WHERE I EXPECT TO FIND
SOMEONE ONLY FOR THE PERSON
NOT TO BE THERE

zerooh

.

HAIKU

Spud Webb, Keith Jennings,
Red Klotz; Slavko Vraneš, Chuck
Nevitt, Sim Bhullar

A CRUCIAL THOUGHT IN DANTE'S LIFE

I like 'em young

.

DESPITE VERTIGO, THIS WAS PROUST'S FAVORITE PLAYGROUND EQUIPMENT

seesaw

HARRY K STAMMER HAS A MOMENT
OF BLISS IN A SUNLIT MEADOW,
THEN HE HAS AN INSTANT OF
LACANIAN PANIC WHEN HE
REALIZES HE IS THE OBJECT OF A
GAZE, THEN HE WELCOMES THE
THUSNESS OF THE UNIVERSE, AND,
LIKE WINNIE-THE-POOH, HUMS A
HUM

doe ray me
fa! so

.

NEIL TO MARK

a northern man
don't need him
around anyhow

A

mead

0?

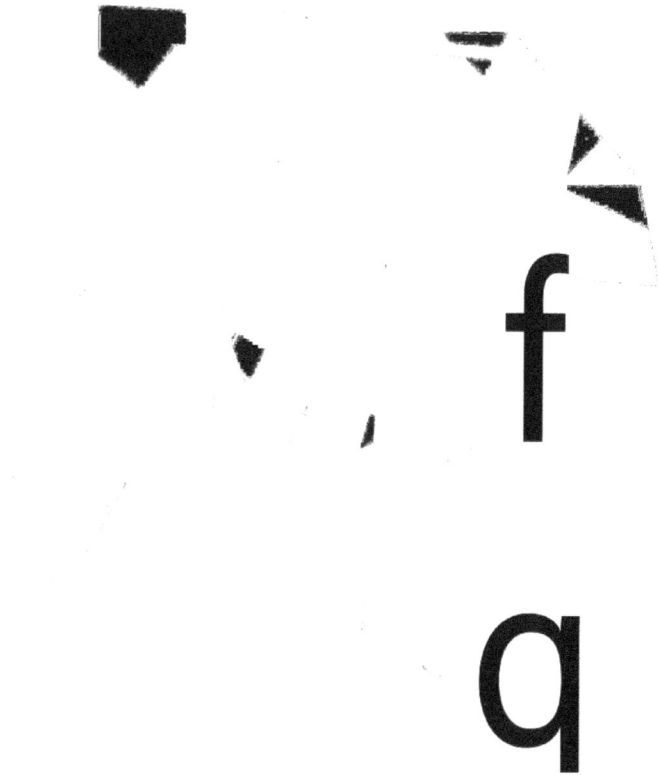

Meanwhile, at the

Typhoon. Gryphon.
Sun's edges set
the sea
inside a lion's
mane. Wings
on the waves,
claws in the sand.

Typo, 'graph.
Signage cites
a scene,
upsets a lying
man. Wife
on the wane,
sand in the wine.

Globe Theatre

Timon of Athens.
The Merchant
of Venice, Love's
Labour's Lost. Titus
Andronicus. The
Merry Wives
of Windsor. Coriolanus.

Time on my hands.
The mired ant.
Oven ice. Elves
lave ears least, tight ass.
End run and kiss the
Mayor. Wise eyes
sufferin' curious love.

French Lemmas

Newest pages ordered by last
category

link update
strepto-
-logiste
pneumothorax
-coque
Mesrine
Bettachini
lacrymo
macronie
zouzou
choupi

Oldest pages ordered by last edit

chien
abime
gratuit
été
CE
webmaster
Fanny
représentant
observateur
gyroscope

Pi

S

tol

Per

R

ier

Pan

Fry

D

ANXIETY OF INFLUENCE

"coffee coffee
coffee coffee"

creamed
creamed

.

PASTORAL (translation)

abcdefghijklmnopqrstUVwxyz

.

DEFINITIVE HISTORY
era sure

irrealevant

.

starveback

But

,
sure
?
and
should it be
arrived in

ˀ
in
is quite
;

fat

ous

*

w **,** mb

*

p•lka

*

Four variations for John Cage

One is not
one. One is.

‡

One is. One
is. Is two.

‡

‡

Two is one.
One is too.

Taken from Pliny,

those lines
of

l
a
n
g
u
o
r
tude &
lassitude.

Spar

K

R

Arrest

ed

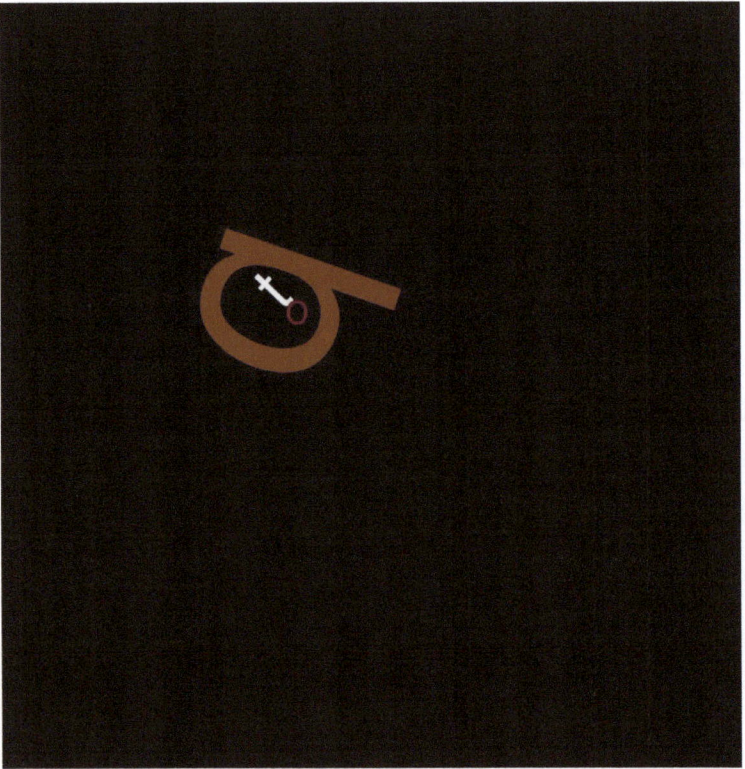

Nor

which

Not I Snot

duhl

.

oblilliterate

.

paranoiache

.

plossibility

LIMITS OF FASHION

peeriod

.

vectar

.

AN ANDY WARHOL BRILLO BOX RECYCLED

snap
crackle
pop

SLIGHTLY SHOCKED

bghast

.

dayliet

.

A LITTLE STRANGE

weeird

.

F0R A MINOR UPSET STOMACH

quantums

SUFFER RING

localeyes
t ouch
queeared
smf'ing'ell
gar lick
se(e)*ms*

.

enteleaky

.

AUTOCORRECT

~~minutes~~
minus

topless

*

fewtoil

*

integʃal

*

fragrancid

*

<u>sk tebo rd</u>
   a   a

*

```
              ^
              b
              i
 <<<<         i         >>>>
              r
              d
              ⚳

              *

            CON
            CRE
            ATE

              *

        theref∴re

              *
```

ru ᚻe

emordnilappalindrome

*

foreignsic

*

prozaic

*

enjamb
ment

*

trespassé

*

To

Tal

Ly

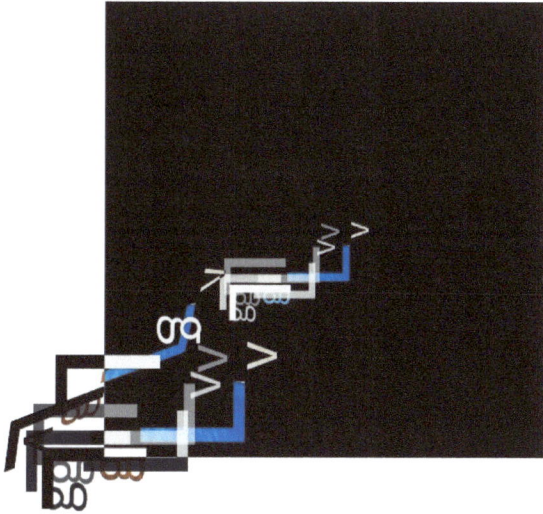

Ne

S

tele

NINE PLUS ONE MORE TO AMUSE JONATHAN WILLIAMS

NARCISSUS

clASSical
is not always as
cLASSical does

.

DAPHNE

her bark
was horrible
but her bite
would have been
a delight

.

A QUIBBLE WITH SILENUS

six inches
is better than
half a foot

.

CASTOR AND POLLUX

embryyo

.

ZEUS AGAIN

cumouflage

.

MOREPHOSIS

my little chickadee

deer
deer

.

HERMAPHRODITUS

asstounding

.

NOT EVERY DAY IS PERFECT

Artemiss
*bore*as
nymth
Apallo
Socratease
symimposium
twerpsichore
perscellphone
Delfie
etHICKS
untrimmed

.

SILENUS WAS RIGHT, BUT

things pass
soon enough
anyway

.

CLAIRE

blond hair
on a Geordie
hiker's calves

À la campagne

School. Public
phone box. Un-
used hall. Over-

grown racetrack.
A gravel road
lies ahead.

Plaint

How
can I
negate my nihils?

it has a certain rhythm to it

which are
from the is

as I
the

*

I wait
with bated
walrus.

s tele

a s unlit
piece
of s tone
p laced
on a h ill side
re counts
t he t ravels

The Complete
Rockhampton Public Library
American Poetry Section

Between *The Poetry
of Robert Frost* & Walt
Whitman's *Leaves of
Grass* — Bette Midler's
The Saga of Baby Divine.

doodle *aka* an / intellectual side / to Lynyrd Skynyrd

Enrolled at the university in Tuscaloosa for several years.

Now about to defend her doctoral thesis.

Formal thesis name:
DEVELOPING A HYBRID BREEDING
SYSTEM TO AVOID OUTBREAKS OF
TURNIP CRINKLE VIRUS (TCV)

Her private name: Swede tome, Alabama.

qro

ket

sere

Co

b

a

in

SMELLS LIKE IT NEEDS MORE TEEN SPIRIT

echocardigan

.

ILLUSION

constrain't

.

enviroffs

ELEGY FOR ALBERT AYLER

b low

.

WANTING IT IS A BIG MISTAKE

nirvanna white

a crocheted embolism

sErRaTe
survive

        poultice
             police

       sentence
           silence

            premise
            promise

            solstice
       solace

            pastiche
       palace

erase
ErRaTa

Scheherazade at the speed of light

The two plays
one novel
&

five
chapters of
autobiography that I

wrote today wouldn't
fit in
this

space
so I'm
leaving it empty.

CARLVONCLAUSEWITZONWAR

EVERYTHEORYBECOMESINFINITELY
MOREDIFFICULTFROMTHEMOMENTTH
ATITTOUCHESONTHEPROVINCEOFMO
RALQUANTITIESARCHITECTUREAND
PAINTINGKNOWQUITEWELLWHATTHE
YAREABOUTEVERYTHEORYBECOMESI
NFINITETASLONGASTHEYHAVEONLY
TODOWITHMATTERTHEREISNODISPU
TEABOUTMECHANICALOROPTICALCO
NSTRUCTIONBUTASSOONASTHEMORA
LACTIVITIESBEGINTHEIRWEVERYT
HEORYBECOMESINFINITEORKASSOO
NASMORALIMPRESSIONSANDFEELIN
GSAREPRODUCEDTHEWHOLESETOFRU
LESDISSOLVESINTOVAGUEIDEASTH
ESCIENCEOFMEDICINEISCHIEFLYE
NGAGEDWI EVERYTHEORYBECOMESI
NFINITETHBODILYPHENOMENAONLY
ITSBUSINESSISWITHTHEANIMALOR
GANISMWHICHLIABLETOPERPETUAL
CHANGEISNEVEREXACTLYTHESAMEF
ORTWOMOMENTSTHISMAKESEVERYTH
EORYBECOMESINFINITEITSPRACTI
CEVERYDIFFICULTANDPLACESTHEJ
UDGEMENTOFTHEPHYSICIANABOVEH
ISSCIENCEBUTHOWMUCHMOREDIFFI
CULTISTHECASEIFAMORALEFFECTI
SADDEDANDHEVERYTHEORYBECOMES
INFINITEOWMUCHHIGHERMUSTWEPL
ACETHEPHYSICIANOFTHEMINDEVER
YTHEORYBECOMESINFINITELYMORE

ne(tar)ne

NOTES

Acknowledgements

Some of Mark Young's poems included here
have previously appeared in

*dadakuku, Lothlorien Poetry Journal, Synchronized
Chaos*, & *Utsanga.it* —
thanks to the respective editors —

& on the *mark young's Series Magritte* & *Won Des
Laits* blog sites.

MORE NOTES

Bios

Mark Cunningham's latest book *gu(e)st (g)host* was also brought out by Sandy Press. Talk about gluttons for punishment.

Mark Young was born in Aotearoa New Zealand but now lives in a small town on traditional Juru land in North Queensland, Australia. He has been publishing poetry for sixty-five years, & is the author of over seventy books, primarily text poetry but also including speculative fiction, vispo, memoir, & art history.

harry k stammer lives in Santa Barbara, CA USA. His books include *tents* – 2007 Otoliths, *grounds* – 2013 Otoliths, *tocsin* – 2019 Otoliths, *-48* – 2021 Sandy Press, *sidewalkss* – 2021 Concrete Mist Press, *walls't's* – 2021 Sandy Press, *alleys't'* – 2023 Concrete Mist Press, and *Getting to One* with Eileen Tabios – 2023 Sandy Press

www.ingramcontent.com/pod-product-compliance
Lightning Source LLC
Chambersburg PA
CBHW041358090426
42741CB00001B/13